Y0-DAE-570

Phonics Fun
Reading Program
Book 11: irregular plurals

Cleo Brushes Her Teeth

by Janelle Cherrington

Illustrated by Gita Lloyd and Eric Binder

Based on the books by Norman Bridwell

SCHOLASTIC INC.
New York Toronto London Auckland Sydney
Mexico City New Delhi Hong Kong Buenos Aires

Cleo was dreaming that she had just found a big bone. She was about to sink her teeth into it when Mrs. Diller woke her up.

"Cleo," Mrs. Diller said, "we must go see Mr. Kibble, the dog groomer, today!"

Oh, no! thought Cleo.

Cleo did not like to go to see Mr. Kibble. He took too long and he puffed her fur too much. *He makes the dogs look like a herd of sheep*, Cleo pouted to herself as she hopped into the car.

"Mrs. Diller," Mr. Kibble began, "I noticed Cleo's breath has been pretty bad lately. You should check with the vet first, but I think you should brush her teeth. I'll do it, if you like."

"Oh, my," said Mrs. Diller. "Let me talk to Dr. Dihn, the vet."

Dr. Dihn agreed with Mr. Kibble. "Teeth brushing is good for dogs," she explained. "Dogs just need a special toothbrush and special toothpaste. The toothpaste doesn't taste like mint leaves. It tastes like meat. I can give them to you."

"Then I'll brush Cleo's teeth right after I brush my own," Mrs. Diller said.

That night, Mrs. Diller brushed her teeth. Cleo ran and hid. Mrs. Diller finally caught up with her and began brushing Cleo's teeth. Cleo shook her head as hard as she could. The toothpaste flew! Mrs. Diller looked like she was wearing a toothpaste suit!

The next day, Cleo told her friends what had happened. "Can you believe it?" she asked.

"I can believe it," Clifford said. "Emily Elizabeth brushes my teeth. I really like it."

"I like it, too," T-Bone added.

"But, but...other animals – like wolves – don't brush their teeth," Cleo said.

"Some other animals – like wolves – aren't as lucky as we are. They don't have owners to care about their health," Clifford said.

That night, Mrs. Diller tried again. Cleo has been smiling ever since.